THE
AMERICAN
DESERT

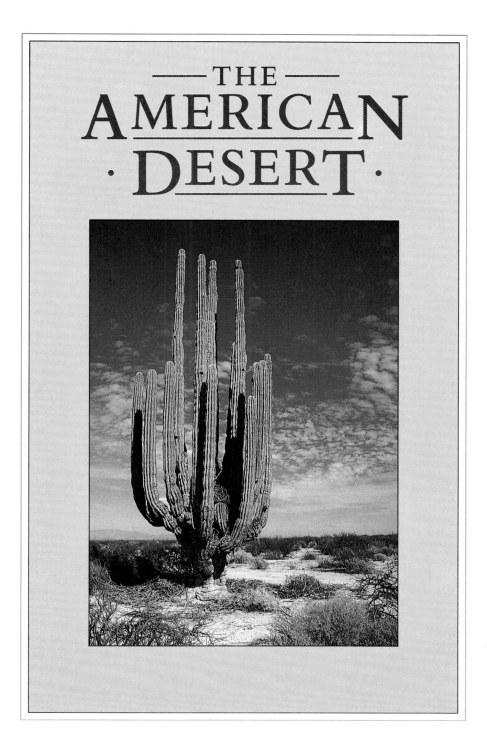

THE
AMERICAN
DESERT

WILLIAM K. HARTMAN

CRESCENT BOOKS
NEW YORK

By the same author: *Desert Heart – Chronicles of the Sonoran Desert*

Featuring the photography of Jeanne Broome,
Gayle Hartmann, William Hartmann, Floyd Herbert,
and Barbara Tellman

CLB 2527
© 1991 Colour Library Books Ltd, Godalming, Surrey, England
All rights reserved
This 1991 edition published by Crescent Books,
distributed by Outlet Book Company, Inc., a Random House Company,
225 Park Avenue South, New York, New York 10003
Printed and bound in Italy
ISBN 0 517 03169 8
8 7 6 5 4 3 2 1

CONTENTS

Previous pages: sunlight and shadows at Zabriskie Point,
Death Valley National Monument, California.
Above: a brief display of desert wildflowers.

PREFACE

Paradoxically, deserts imply perilous travel, and yet exercise a curious attraction. The beauty of these regions is unique, with strange plants and lonely vistas often ringed by blue mountains. This beauty is fragile; a disturbance is not readily covered by new plant growth because the plant cover is sparse, and the life cycles of change are slow; a combination that is exerting more and more influence on American national life as people move from the populous east and west coasts into the more pristine environments

of the desert west. One the one hand, this means that more and more people are enjoying the mystique and the spectacular scenery of the American deserts. On the other, it mean that there is more and more stress on these fragile environments. This book provides an introduction to the beauty, fragility, and environmental challenges offered by the American deserts, in the belief that greater knowledge of place leads to greater enjoyment and care.

Above: flowering Prickly Pear cactus in Capitol Reef National Park, Utah.
Facing page: snowfall in the Rincon foothills, New Mexico.

Death Valley at dusk shows the effect of lack of water – the defining characteristic of a desert.

1

What Makes a Desert?

From *The Thousand and One Nights*, to the film *Lawrence of Arabia*, many images have helped foster our conception of a desert. At first, the idea of a desert seems clear enough. The very term conjures up images of sand dunes, and desolate wastelands. Yet defining what makes a desert has several layers of subtlety.

A desert is defined primarily by lack of water. The other properties follow from this. Lack of water implies a relatively sparse ground cover: small, scrubby plants or no plants at all. In the absence of plants, wind can dislodge soil particles and move them around, sculpting peculiar rock forms unknown in other areas, and causing sand grains to accumulate in dunes.

Contrary to common conception, "desert" does not necessarily imply great heat. Equatorial deserts, such as the Sahara, may be very hot. Low altitude deserts such as the Mojave Desert of California may be very hot in the summer and cool in the winter. The dry desert lands of Eastern

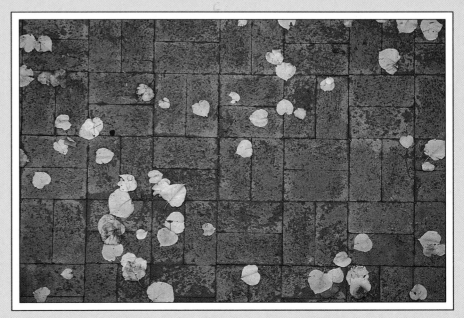

Apricot leaves on a home patio – an attractive pattern of fall in desert cities.

Dry arroyos and erosion forms are the result of erosion processes in arid regions. West of Capitol Reef National Monument, Utah.

Oregon have a relatively cool climate. High latitudes may produce cold deserts. The so-called dry valleys of Antarctica, marked by gravel and rock deposits among snowy mountains, are technically deserts. Even the planet Mars has primarily desert landscapes, with common desert features such as dunes, dust devils, and dry river channels!

At a second level of subtlety, factors like seasonal distribution of rainfall and the rate of evaporation come into play. For example, a strong concentration of rain in only one season may foster certain plants, but only those desert varieties that can survive through the dry spell that lasts the rest of the year. On the other hand, the same amount of rain evenly distributed among the months may allow patchy grasses or low bushes to thrive. Similarly, a cool region with ten inches of rainfall may allow the water to sink into the ground and support substantial plant communities, but in a very hot region with the same rainfall, the rain evaporates rapidly upon hitting the ground, without leaving enough for plants. In turn, latitude, surrounding mountains, and distance from the sea may control the factors of rainfall timing and evaporation rate. The nature of the soil may also control how much water it can hold for plants. Thus, even though a desert is defined by its dryness (not its heat), we cannot easily predict desert conditions, appearance, or vegetation types from annual rainfall figures alone.

Rainstorm in the Sonoran Desert, Arizona.

Colorful strata, Cedar Breaks National Monument, Utah.

Eroded stream channel in sandstone. Arches National Park, Utah.

Sun-baked mud has cracked and curled in a dry wash at Grand Falls, near Flagstaff, Arizona.

Sunset and storm over the Grand Canyon.

Flash flood fills a normally dry wash and spills over into surrounding land.
The wash may be dry again in an hour. Arches National Park, Utah.

Art critic John Van Dyke wrote that a desert sunset in a
clear sky was the most sublime sunset of all.

Sunset light on eroded sandstone cliffs in Arches National Monument, Utah.

2

Deserts of the United States

The deserts of the United States are a phenomenon of the West. Deserts representing different vegetation and climate types stretch almost continuously from west Texas, across southern New Mexico and Arizona and up into southeastern California, Utah, Nevada, and north to the boundary of eastern Oregon with southwest Idaho. Some geographers include the western borderlands of Colorado and Wyoming in their definition of desert. Of all the states, Nevada is the only one occupied almost entirely by desert – a fact which correlates with Nevada's extremely low population density.

These desert regions are divided into four zones with surprisingly distinctive vegetation, wildlife, and climate. These zones comprise the four great deserts of America. Easternmost is the Chihuahuan Desert, extending across west Texas, southern New Mexico, and far south across the Mexican state of Chihuahua and down the central axis of Mexico.

A tourist gives scale to the impressive Double Arch, Arches National Park, Utah.

Counting its Mexican extension, the Chihuahuan Desert is the largest in North America, with an area of about 175,000 square miles. Only a relatively small part lies in the United States, however. The Chihuahuan is a highland desert, associated with the high plains of the Rocky Mountain spine of western North America. Elevations range up to about 5000 feet in the United States with the lowest portions being along the Rio Grande valley at about 1000 feet. Soils are rich in calcium minerals, and include the famous dunes of White Sands National Monument in New Mexico. These white dunes are rich in the white mineral gypsum, or hydrated calcium sulfate. The rainfall comes primarily in brief but violent summer storms, when moist air systems from the Gulf of Mexico push northwest across the region. Rainfall averages around ten inches per year.

West of the Chihuahuan Desert, across the southern Rockies and the Sierra Madre Occidental in Mexico, lies the Sonoran Desert. This is a low, hot desert, but strangely it has a greater diversity of plant and animal species than the other deserts, because of its subtropical climate and the fact that it gets both summer rains (from the Gulf of Mexico) and gentler winter rains (in weather systems pushing down from the north). The Sonoran Desert is marked by a variety f soil and rock types, including many sites of geologically young volcanic eruptions. The youngest is probably Sunset Crater in Arizona, which erupted in A.D. 1066, and probably as recently as 1250. The Sonoran Desert spreads across southwest Arizona and just across the Colorado River into California; it also extended south into Mexico, down both sides of the Gulf of California.

To the northwest, the Sonoran Desert grades into the Mojave Desert, associated primarily with southeast California. This is the smallest of the four desert areas in the United States, covering only 54,000 square miles. The Mojave is a low desert, occupying the mostly-dry basin that extends the Gulf of California trough northwestward into the United

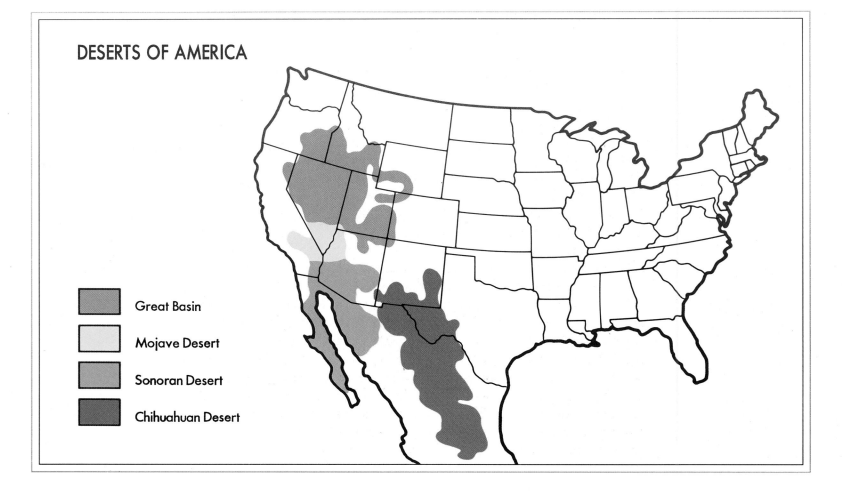

DESERTS OF AMERICA

Great Basin

Mojave Desert

Sonoran Desert

Chihuahuan Desert

Long vistas with sparse ground vegetation are typical of the Great Basin, as in this view in Canyonlands National Park, Utah.

States. Among its famous low spots is Death Valley National Monument, California, which reaches 282 feet below sea level. Summer temperatures in the Mojave are included the highest in the United States, commonly reaching 120°F, and rising to the maximum ever recorded in the United States – 134°F in Death Valley. Rainfall is correspondingly low, typically four or five inches per year.

North and east of the Mojave Desert stretches the largest desert wholly within the United States, the Great Basin Desert. Though largest, the Great Basin Desert is relatively unrecognized because it has the least exotic vegetation and landscapes, lacking the most dramatic cacti and yucca of the other deserts. Much of this desert lies at a relatively high altitude, around 4000 feet, in valleys separated by long mountain ridges.

The four deserts of the United States cover some 300,000 square miles. This comprises only eight percent of the nation's land area, but at the same time it is an exotic, forbidding jewel, set in more familiar surroundings where the early European settlers felt at home. Today, this eight percent of the country provides not only many parklands and spectacular vistas for visitors, but also a haven of increasing attraction, drawing retirees and other settlers tired of the cold, snow, rain and humidity of other regions. These new settlers of the late twentieth century experience an unusual environment with many pleasures and a great sense of openness, but they are also stewards of the most fragile part of the country.

Desert hiker's paradise: Mooney Falls, Havasu Canyon, a branch of the Grand Canyon. Havasu Indian Reservation, Arizona.

Grand Canyon, Arizona.

The Saguaro cactus is the hallmark of the Sonoran Desert, shown here with spring flowers near Tucson, Arizona.

Reflected desert light gives vivid color to the underside of Landscape Arch, Arches National Park, Utah.

Wooded groves along desert streams are known by the Spanish term, *bosque*. Canelo Hills, southeast Arizona.

Ubehebe Crater is an extinct volcano in Death Valley National Monument. Its walls of adobe-like volcanic soil display striking erosion patterns.

Distant horizons and afternoon storms often produce spectacular thunderhead clouds in the deserts of the Southwest. Grand Canyon, Arizona.

Sunlight picks out a distant cliff seen from the Kaibab Trail, Grand Canyon National Park.

Late afternoon in the Mojave Desert, east of Death Valley, California.

Saguaro National Monument, Tucson, Arizona.

Grasslands and a Mesquite tree on the lower slopes of the Catalina Mountains, Arizona. Each elevation zone in the desert mountains has its own plant and animal community.

A snowy morning in the desert. The Sonoran Desert of south-central Arizona gets an average of one or two snowfalls a year. The distant knobby peak is Baboquivari, sacred mountain of the Tohono O'dham Indians.

3

Climate and Geology of the Desert

Deserts have a number of interesting climatic and geologic features not found in more clement regions. Generally, the air is very clear because of the low humidity and generally low air pollution levels. For this reason, one can see unusually large distances, and the horizon is often rimmed by distant mountains, colored deep sky-blue by the light scattered in the atmosphere along the long line of sight.

The temperature difference between day and night in the desert is much greater than in other regions. This is another consequence of the dry air. Because of this dry, clear air, the sunlight heats the ground strongly during the day, rising rapidly from cool dawn temperatures to warm afternoons. A desert dweller learns to dress in layers, shedding a sweater perhaps by noon, depending on the season, but donning it again in the evening. At night, the ground radiates the heat back into the dark sky, cooling the air dramatically. This re-radiation is called infrared radiation, and due to an infrared-absorbing property of water vapor molecules, in humid regions the re-radiated heat is absorbed by the air. Therefore, in

Once the desert ground cover of plants is disturbed (as, in this case, by military maneuvers) the wind can quickly raise the dust, and erosion begins.

such humid regions the night temperature stays much closer to the day temperature – much warmer – than the night temperature in the desert. It is not uncommon for a camping party to be hot in the desert daytime, only to have their water freeze at night.

Two ghostly apparitions of the desert – *mirages* and *dust devils* – arise from associated processes. Under a clear sky, desert soils get very hot on summer afternoons when the sun is high. The hot soil heats the air close to the ground. This creates a strong difference in temperature and optical properties between the air near the ground and the air a few feet above that. The strong gradient in the air's optical properties can make the sheet of air at ground level reflect like a mirror, creating a mirage – the illusion of an expanse of water.

The hot air masses heated by the ground tend to rise for the same reason that a hot air balloon rises. Air rarely rises in a direct, vertical motion, but rather picks up eddies and swirls. The consequence is one of the most ghostly apparitions of a desert – the dust devil. A dust devil is a

The Colorado River has cut beautiful canyon cliffs not only in the Grand Canyon itself, but along other parts of its length, such as this stretch in Utah.

column of swirling dust and light debris picked up by ascending masses of hot air.

Winds play a strong role in shaping desert landscapes, because there are so few plants to hold the soil down; soils and sands are moved by the vagaries of the wind. Of course, the most famous result is dunes. If you think about it, dunes are strange: why shouldn't the wind deposit blowing sand uniformly or at random, instead of piling it in one spot and clearing it in another? One way dunes accumulate is that a given sand grain tends to blow along until it hits a pile of grains; so that if a single pile starts anywhere at random, it tends to grow. Dunes themselves are in slow motion, as the wind whips grains up the windward slope, and off the top onto the leeward slope. So, during months or years, the dune shifts position.

Dunes have different forms, depending on the nature of the winds. Some desert regions have very strong prevailing winds that blow always from the same direction. Other desert regions may have winds from one direction in one season, and another direction in another season.

Sand grains saltating across the tops of dunes in Monument Valley, Utah.

Depending on such differences, dune shapes may be long, straight, parallel ridges, crescents, or overlapping wave forms mixed together.

When the wind blows, small sand grains are picked up, while heavier grains do not move so easily. If you trace the motions of an individual grain, you find that is hops along the surface in a motion called *saltation*. It gets lofted by one gust of wind, rises a foot or so, but then falls back, only to be picked up again. Smaller grains rise higher, larger grains stay near the ground. The net result is that a windstorm produces a strong layer of blowing sand, usually concentrated in the first foot of so above the ground; the same effect is often a nuisance at a sandy beach, where you feel your ankles being "sandblasted," and where the sand blows in your face when you lie down. In the same way, rocks and cliffs in desert areas often experience extreme erosion in the first foot or so above ground level. Driving through very barren desert areas, you will often see rocks and cliffs that appear to be undercut; they will have a cave-like overhang eroded into their lowest foot or so, due to centuries of sandblasting by this effect.

Desert soils are strikingly different from soils in moist regions, due to effects of evaporation. Water in any soil dissolves certain minerals, often called salts. These include true salt (sodium chloride) but also other chlorides, carbonates, etc. If you take a drop of salty water and let it evaporate on your tabletop, it will leave a white deposit, because the salt molecules are left behind as the water molecules go off in the air. In the same way salts are left behind in desert soils as the water evaporates after every rain. As a result, desert soils build up a tremendous concentration of hard, salty deposits. The most famous is called hardpan or *Caliche* (ca-lee'-chee) – usually encountered as one or more layers, about half an inch thick, of whitish calcium carbonate mineral just under the surface of the ground. It is the bane of desert gardeners, being very hard to break through with a shovel.

Desert basins are sites of the strongest deposits of salts and caliche because rainstorm water runs off the hills, collects in temporary lakes, and then these lakes evaporate, leaving salts. The resultant soils get saltier over the centuries, until no plants can grow in them. These broad, flat, lakebed deposits are called *playas*, from the Spanish for beaches, and they range from a hundred yards to a mile or more in size, being prominent, bright, sterile patches as seen from the air.

Strata of different strengths have produced strangely eroded rocks in Goblin Valley State Park, Utah.

Havasu Canyon, one of the most beautiful side canyons branching off the Grand Canyon, offers turquoise-colored waters and stunning waterfalls. Havasu Indian Reservation, Arizona.

The migration of sand dunes. Wind blows sand up the shallow slope of the dune and over its lip, eventually moving the crest of the dune forward. The individual sand grains are picked up by the wind, dropped, and picked up again – a hopping motion called saltation.

Late afternoon in the dunes, Death Valley National Monument, California.

Afternoon storm clouds build up over mountain ranges in the Southwest deserts in August, when seasonal winds bring moist air from the Gulf of Mexico.

Green plants crowd a ledge where water seeps out of a
sandstone formation. Zion National Park, Utah.

Banded granitic boulders make patterns of light and dark in the afternoon sun.
Rock declivities catch water and create attractive microenvironments in desert mountains. Catalina Mountains, Arizona.

Aravaipa Canyon.

One of the most unusual features of the American deserts is Meteor Crater, Arizona, where a large meteorite blasted a crater over half a mile wide.

Landscape Arch, nearly 300 feet long, is one of many extraordinary landforms in Arches National Park, Utah. The sandstone units were fractured by parallel vertical fracture planes, and eventually some of the resultant tabular rock cliffs were eroded into arches.

Streamline flow deposit of sediments in Bill Williams Wash, western Arizona.

The "Devil's Golf Course" is a region of salt deposits caused by evaporation in Death Valley, California.

Eroded sediments, Zabriskie Point, Death Valley National Monument.

4

Geology Shapes the Desert

The portions of the American west occupied by the desert are mostly part of a broad part of the continent that geologists call the basin and range province. The name comes from the arrangement of the topography in craggy, low mountain ridges, usually running northwest-to-southeast, separated by shallow valleys some miles or tens of miles wide. Nevada in particular is a heartland of this region, but it can be seen in parts of all four American deserts – Great Basin (named for this type of topography), Sonoran, Mojave, and Chihuahuan.

Production of the basin and range region involved interesting planetary-scale geologic forces. According to the theories of plate tectonics, developed in recent decades, the earth's crustal layers (some tens of miles thick) form relatively rigid "plates" floating on hotter, sluggishly-flowing, partly melted material. Western North America is a zone where the underlying currents are pulling the surface layers apart,

The Box Elder tree is named for its common occurrence in box canyons.
Burr Trail near Capitol Reef, Utah.

Spider Rock, a spectacular eroded remnant in Canyon de Chelly, Arizona.

from east to west. Earthquakes are the frequent results, as these forces cause the more rigid rocks to crack, pulling apart a little at a time or sliding past each other. Slowly, over the centuries, these movements are pulling Baja California and the California coast away from the mainland. This stretching of the desert west broke the crust into parallel ridges and valleys – the Basin and Range Province – dotting it with black lava flows where molten magma reached the surface.

There are some easy principles that explain much of the topography in the desert West. The two most important principles are that there are few plants to hold the soil, and what little rain that falls is often concentrated in strong storms that run dry washes into raging torrents for just a few days. These two factors produce certain characteristic erosion patterns that are repeated throughout many desert landscapes, and are quite different from the rolling hills, gentle valleys, and meandering streams that characterize the more wooded uplands of the continent.

In the first place, the mountain ridges, lacking a protective blanket of forests to hold the soil, are eroded down to their most resistant, craggy rocks – the bony skeletons of the desert Earth. Weaker soils and rock particles that have washed away from the stark ridges are moved down to the low flanks of the mountains, where the flatter desert begins. As the cascading waters fan out into the desert, they slow, lose their erosive power, and drop their load of eroded sediment. Abroad, gentle slope of only a few degrees therefore fans out around the base of each mountain. Such an apron is called a *bajada*, from the Spanish for slope.

Chiracahua Mountains, southeast Arizona.

An azure circular lake fills the crater of a small volcanic cone at Zuni Salt Lake,
New Mexico.

Many mountain ranges of the desert Southwest are National Forest lands, and offer striking vistas and welcome
hiking trails for desert dwellers. Huachuca Mountains, Coronado National Forest, Arizona.

The erosive process, while wearing down a mountain, may expose a flat stratum of very strong rock, such as an ancient lava flow. This layer is called cap rock and tends to protect the underlying strata from erosion. This situation produces towering, flat-topped buttes, such as the famous examples in Monument Valley on the eastern Utah-Arizona border, the region where Hollywood directors filmed several classic Western movies. A broader layer of cap rock can protect a large elevated region, called a *mesa*, from the Spanish term for table.

Geologic forces may uplift and tilt a broad region. Rivers that had been sluggish now run faster down the resulting slopes, causing severe erosion. Deep canyons can be cut. This was the history of the Colorado River as it cut across the broad, uplifted region called the Colorado Plateau, in northern Arizona. The result was that the river cut the Grand Canyon, exposing deep, ancient rock layers, and producing world-famous vistas.

Certain micro-environments offer a variety in the desert. Where river or spring water produces a high water table, swamp-like ponds become refuges for wildlife. They are known by the Spanish term, *cienega*. This one is in the Sonoran Desert of Southern Arizona.

Sunset light catches streamers of virga (rain that evaporates before hitting the ground,) Monument Valley, Utah.

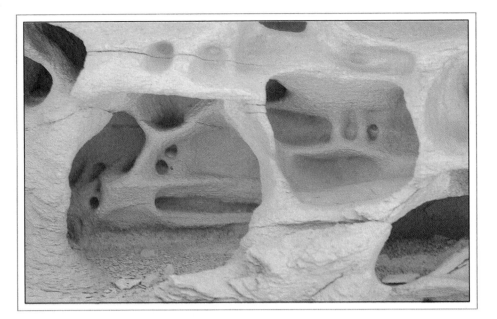

Erosion processes cause strange rock formations. Wapatki National Monument, Arizona.

Navajo Loop Trail, Zion National Park, Utah.

Rocky debris in the foreground hints at the erosive process by which the cliff faces collapse and leave a flat-topped butte as a final remnant. Southeast Utah.

Spring flowers grace the bajada at the foot of Picaho Peak, Arizona.

Bone-like granite ridges seem almost sterile in contrast to the saguaros and other plants of the desert floor. Cabeza Prieta National Wildlife Refuge, Arizona.

Cottonwoods add a lush green to the redrock country of Canyon de Chelly, Arizona.

Kaibab Trail, Grand Canyon National Park, Arizona.

Cliffs and towers are formed as sandstone units are eroded down to their last, resistant remnants. Arches National Park, Utah.

The basin and range country of Utah offers many contrasts between fertile valleys and barren cliffs.

A mesa near Capitol Reef National Park, Utah.

Spider Rock is a remnant left by erosion in the middle of Canyon de Chelly, Arizona.

Spider Rock is a towering remnant left as streams eroded channels through a rock stratum at Canyon de Chelly, Arizona.

A plucky desert plant gains a foothold
on dunes in Monument Valley, Utah.

Delicate Arch, one of the most picturesque features in Arches National Park, Utah.

Eroded pediments, Death Valley National Monument, California.

Grand Canyon, Arizona.

Dusk in the dune fields of Death Valley, California,
one of the most arid regions within the Mojave Desert.

Flat-topped buttes are a signature of Monument Valley, on the Utah-Arizona border, where many Western films were shot.

Sand Verbena forms a transient lavender carpet on the desert floor.

5

Plants and Animals of the Desert

While the woodlands of the American East, South, and Northwest impress us with life at its most luxuriant, the deserts impress us no less with the opposite aspect of biology. Desert life shows the sheer tenacity of the life process. Humans may die after only a few days exposure in the desert, but many plants and animals have evolved and adapted for fit desert conditions. One striking example is found in the forms of leaves. In heavily forested areas, leaves are broad and flat, lazily unfolding the maximum possible green surface area to the sun in order to accomplish photosynthesis at a maximum rate. Because life is so profligate in those climates, trees stretch to outdo each other, reaching extreme heights to get their leaves above the rest of the forest canopy. In the deserts, away from streambeds, leaves have an entirely different character. They are as small as possible, to minimize evaporation of precious water from the plant through the leaf surface into the dry air. For the same reason, desert leaves often have a waxy or

Datura is a hallucinogenic plant that is common in the Sonoran Desert.

Lichens and ferns are common in the mountains of the desert southwest.

oily coating, which protects against rapid evaporation. Desert trees are spaced well apart, because there is only a little water to be shared among root systems. A new shoot growing too close to an established tree will not be able to compete for moisture with the established root system. Probably for this reason, desert trees do not grow to great heights: they don't have to compete for sunlight. The tiny leaves of trees such as the mesquite or palo verde are bunched, many to a stem, in order to get enough surface area to allow photosynthesis. In cacti, the leaves are replaced by thorns, which protect against animals who would forage for the moist pulp inside the pant. Cacti and some trees such as the palo verde, having de-emphasized leaves to a greater or lesser extent, have chlorophyll in their bark or stalk, explaining their green color. *Palo verde* means "green stick" in Spanish, an apt description of the green branches and trunk.

The American deserts support an astonishing variety of plants and animals. This surprises many newcomers, who expect less vigorous biology in a more extreme environment. But nature tends to crowd variety into environments where there are "contact zones," or contacts between one micro-environment and another. A forest may have many miles of relatively uniform terrain, but in twenty miles of desert, we find broad, dry, sandy zones, a wash that may be flooded three times a year, a mountain range with winter snow, a rocky ridge with a spring seeping out of its base, and an eruption of volcanic ash. While the desert expanses have fearsome cacti, the streambeds may be lined by lush, green cottonwood trees, which turn gold in the fall. Each of these zones produces its own soils, moisture level, and climate, as well as its own clustering of bushes, lichens, birds, lizards, cacti, trees, and other species.

Prickly poppy seeds have lain dormant in a mud playa, but spring to life after a storm whose water has already evaporated. Sonora, Mexico.

Desert plants appear in unlikely places when a rainy season causes dormant seeds to sprout. Capitol Reef National Monument, Utah.

Of course, hundreds of species of plants and animals can be found in each of the four American deserts, but a few species of plants stand out as "signature" plants of each. In the Chihuahuan Desert, one of the most characteristic plants is the creosote, a scrubby bush about the height of a person. It is not visually striking, but its tiny, oily leaves give off a welcome, pungent odor when dampened by rain. As an aromatic harbinger of the return of the wetter seasons, the plant is a favorite of southwest residents.

In the Sonoran Desert, the creosote is still common, but the "signature" plant is the stately saguaro cactus, rising tens of feet, and shown off in the fantastic landscapes of Saguaro National Monument,

Grassland on high plains of the Sonoran Desert, near Sonora, Arizona.

near Tucson, Arizona. The tallest of these may be more than 150 years old. The Sonoran Desert has some of the most weirdest and most unfamiliar plants, as judged by visitors. Among the saguaros may be found the green-barked palo verde tree, the ocotillo, which looks like a bunch of thorny sticks gathered at the bottom, and a variety of small cacti including the prickly pear, barrel, and teddy-bear. The latter looks almost furry, but a hiker who brushes against it even slightly is likely to come away with a piece of the fragile stalk stuck to his arm or leg by a dozen very painful thorns.

"Signature plants" of the Mojave Desert include various yuccas, which have a cluster of low, blade-like leaves, surmounted by a tall,

flowering stalk that may rise 10 to 17 feet. largest of the yuccas is the Joshua tree, rising 15 to 30 feet in a striking, forked structure crowned by clumps of sword-like leaves. It is seen to good advantage at Joshua Tree National Monument, California.

The Great Basin Desert, though the largest in the United States, is usually regarded as the least picturesque in terms of plants. Its broad landscapes are dotted by modest, bushy sagebrush, along with various grasses and other low bushes.

Characteristic animal species are more broadly spread across the deserts. One of the best known is the coyote, resembling a dog but usually somewhat leaner and more alert. Coyotes range across most of the west and into Canada, and are widely known in western Indian mythology, usually as a playful trickster. In modern American cartoon mythology, Wily Coyote chases the roadrunner, a striking bird seen frequently along highways in the southern half of the West. The roadrunner feeds on lizards and insects, and while it sometimes flies short distances, it more characteristically runs along the ground.

Most first-time desert visitors are frightened by reports of snakes, scorpions, tarantulas, Gila Monsters and other noxious creatures. Considering the distribution of various species of poisonous rattlesnakes, including the Western, the Western Diamondback, the Mojave, and the Sidewinder, one can encounter a rattlesnake in practically any part of the four deserts. Although such encounters are rare, one must be on the lookout. The most important rule is never to step or reach into a spot that you cannot see, such as the far side of a rock or log. Fatal bites are rare, but occur usually when on has accidentally intruded into the snake's space. Given warning, the snake usually rattles and may retreat. Similarly, to avoid scorpions, the important rule is not to pick up rocks or pieces of wood without examining the underside first, since scorpions typically hide under such objects. As for tarantulas, they are more fearsome in appearance and size than they are dangerous. And Gila Monsters, which range primarily through western Arizona, are very rare. This thick-bodied lizard is usually sluggish unless deliberately provoked.

The Barrel cactus has spectacular red flowers.

Butterflies make a brief visit on a sunflower.

Nightblooming cereus makes a spectacular blossom that shrivels in the desert sun.

Prickly Pear cacti with ripe fruit. Following native tradition, modern Sonoran Desert dwellers pick the fruit to make jelly and candies.

Throughout the desert southwest, rocky canyons in mountain foothills are often scenes of vigorous life that is supported by water runoff from the hills above. The Cottonwood tree shown here is common in the Sonoran Desert, and a beautiful sight as its leaves turn gold in the fall.

Manzanita bark offers striking contrasts of red and gray.

The homely but aromatic Creosote Bush perfumes the desert air after each rain in the Chihuahuan and Sonoran deserts.

The soft-looking "fuzz" on Teddy Bear Cholla is actually composed of innumerable vicious spines. Picacho State Park, Arizona.

Fleabane flowers in a beautiful setting against red
sandstone in Capitol Reef National Park, Utah.

The grandest tree of the desert southwest is the Cottonwood, which turns resplendent gold in the fall. New Mexico.

Yellow Senecio flowers and white composites bring
May color to the desert in northwest Arizona.

Cactus blossoms, Arizona.

Arizona poppy.

The Bristlecone Pine lives to very great age, and its rings were critical in establishing the tree ring patterns that allow archaeologists to date ancient timbers. Cedar Breaks National Monument, southwestern Utah.

A Joshua Tree and low brush are characteristic of the Mojave Desert. West of China Lake, California.

Indian Paint Brush adds a splash of color along desert mountain trails.

Thistle blossom, Zion Narrows Trail, Zion National Park, Utah.

The Joshua Tree is a signature plant of the Mojave Desert. Near China Lake, California.

Lichens in Tsegi Canyon, Arizona.

The furry appearance of vicious thorns, when seen at a distance, gives the Teddy Bear Cholla cactus its name.

A bee visits Saguaro blossoms in a play of light and shade.

Prickly Pear cactus blossom near Tucson, in the Sonoran Desert.

A backlit thistle makes a dramatic sight in Olsen Wash, Arizona.

Brittle Bush and Senita Pinacate.

Rocky Mountain Phlox on the Grand Canyon's South Rim, Arizona.

Lupine

Scrubby vegetation in the plateau country of Great Basin National Park, Nevada.

Prickly Pear cactus bud and blossom, Arizona.

Snow and ice coat the thorns of a Cholla cactus on a wintry morning in the Sonoran Desert, southern Arizona.

Buds form a characteristic crown on the Barrel Cactus, Sonoran Desert.

A contrast of soil types and plants. Sandy dry soil in the foreground supports scrubby
Creosote Bushes; basalt lava hill in the background supports almost no large plants.

The thick leaves of the Agave, a succulent in the Sonoran Desert, form interesting patterns.

A dramatic radial pattern of Yucca leaves, Sonoran Desert, southern Arizona.

A Yucca stalk in the Chihuahuan Desert, western New Mexico.

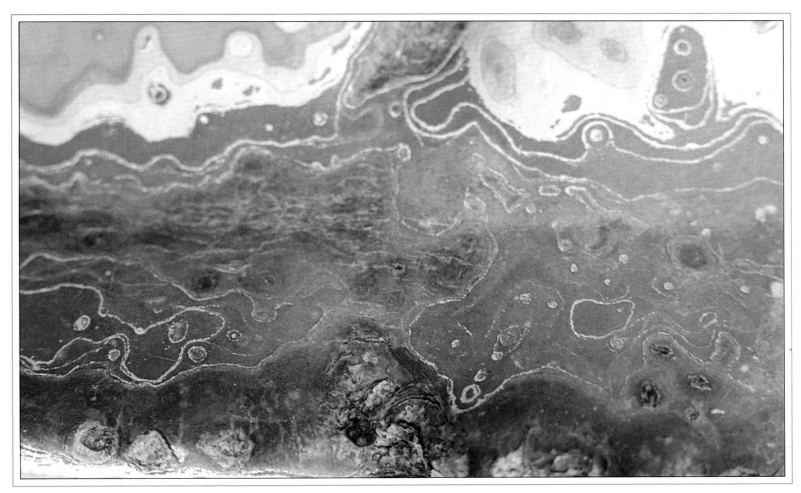

An interesting abstract pattern is made by a few inches of the green skin of a Saguaro cactus. Sonora, Mexico.

Baby Great-horned Owls, on display at the Arizona-Sonora Desert Museum, Tucson Arizona.

▲ Red-tailed Hawk.

▲ Rock Squirrel in Picacho Peak State Park, Arizona.

The real Road Runner is almost as feisty as its cartoon version.

The Harris Hawk is found in scattered populations
across all four American deserts.

A Clark's Nutcrackers, Bryce Canyon National Park, Utah.

The Gray Fox is found in both the Sonoran and Chihuahuan deserts.

Prairie Dogs keep vigilant watch at their burrow entrances.

Hualapai Canyon, Havasu Indian Reservation, Arizona.

Due to its large size and hairy covering, the Tarantula
looks more fearsome than it really is.

A harmless lizard strikes a fearsome pose in the Saguaro National
Monument of the Sonoran Desert, near Tucson, Arizona.

Rattlesnake in Zion National Park, Utah.

Tarantula, Cabeza Prieta National Wildlife Refuge, southwest Arizona.

The sluggish Gila Monster, named for the Gila River, is one of only two species of venomous lizard .

The White House Ruin was inhabited a thousand years ago. Canyon de Chelly, Arizona.

6

Native
Americans
of the Deserts

Almost ghostly in their background presence are the deserts' Native Americans, both prehistoric and modern. Their life is one of the desert's most interesting aspects for several reasons. First, of all the ancient cultures of the United States, the most artistically sophisticated and technically advanced lived in the desert Southwest. Second, better than any other climate, the dry desert has preserved vestiges of the ancient peoples. Third, Indian cultures of the area today have experienced a renaissance in artistic craftsmanship.

Controversy surrounds the Indians' arrival from Asia. Across the continent, and especially in the desert, ancient campsites are found dating back 12,000 years. Humans were clearly in the West at that time, and most archaeologists think these were the first Americans. But in recent years, archaeologists tramping the forbidding back country of the Sonoran and Mojave deserts have found sites with very crude tools, possibly dating to 20,000 or 30,000 years ago. While some scientists question the validity of these sites, others are beginning to believe that a few hardy settlers

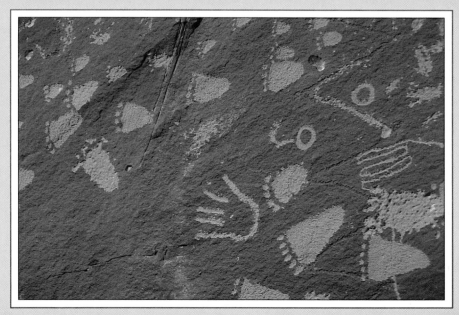

An ancient Indian, perhaps with a sense of humor, "pecked" these footprints across a rock cliff face in Utah.

Bedrock mortar holes are common near desert water sources.
Prehistoric Indians made them for grinding food.

came across the Bering Sea ice pack that long ago, only to be followed near the close of the last ice age by a larger mass migration about 12,000 years ago.

Prehistoric cultures in the Sonoran and Chihuahuan deserts rose to the highest levels, in terms of buildings, irrigation systems, and art. Probably they were influenced by the still great Mesoamerican cultures in central Mexico, with whom they traded. Whatever the influence, by around A.D. 800 to 1400 they were building multi-story buildings of stone or adobe, free-standing or built into the cliffs. Their main towns were along the rivers winding through these regions, such as the Rio Grande in New Mexico and the Gila and Salt in Arizona. Oval ball courts, resembling small football stadiums, were common in these towns, and attest to a sport that was imported from Mexico. In these settlements, prehistoric people made striking turquoise jewelry, complex irrigation canal systems, and beautifully painted pots, whose fragments are still found today. Of the passions that ruled their lives, we know almost nothing.

Something happened around A.D. 1200-1400. We know there were widespread climate changes in America at this time (the Vikings had to pull out of America and Greenland, too). Whether due to climate change, agricultural failures, movements of peoples, or decline of the influential civilizations to the south, the patterns of housing and art changed. By 1450, hardly any painted pottery was being made in the deserts, making it difficult for archaeologists to identify and trace cultural relationships from one village to another.

Around 1900, however, American traders developed a market for modern Indian crafts, including jewelry, rugs, and ceramics based loosely on the prehistoric designs, and encouraged the Indians to revive ancient skills. The principle areas of modern production are on the northern fringes of the Chihuahuan and Sonoran deserts, especially among the various pueblo tribes of northern New Mexico and the Navajo and Hopi of northern Arizona. In these areas, many Indians choose to continue life in the picturesque style that echoes ancient traditions, such as the multi-story pueblos of New Mexico, or the hogans of Arizona. In other desert regions, Indians have been resettled into modern government houses, many of which seems to lack the insulation and shade needed to be environmentally suited to the region.

Some of the most spectacular Indian cliff dwellings in Arizona are at Canyon de Chelly. This is Antelope House Ruin.

T-shaped doorways were common in prehistoric Southwest cliff dwellings, such as this example in Grand Gulch, Utah.

Prehistoric Indian rock painting, Grand Gulch, Utah.

Prehistoric Indians, probably around A.D. 1000, utilized sandstone cliffs as their canvases. Grand Gulch, Utah.

Prehistoric Indian petroglyphs, probably ca. A.D. 100, southern Arizona.

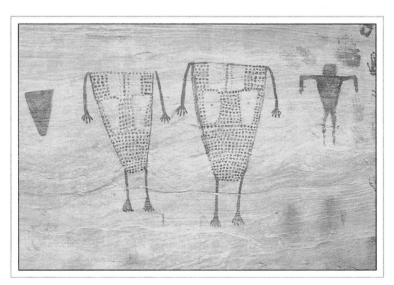

"Thunderbird" and other motifs on prehistoric Indian petroglyphs, southern Arizona.

Canyon de Chelly, Arizona.

An early rancher incorporated prehistoric Indian grinding stones into the
wall around the door of this ranchhouse. Baboquivari Ranch, southern Arizona.

Wapatki National Monument, Arizona, contains several prehistoric Indian dwellings.

Prehistoric Indian trails leading across the desert are well preserved because of lack of erosion and lack of disturbance by vegetation.

Broken shells far from the sea among basalt cobbles in the Aguila Mountains of Arizona mark ancient Indian activity. Indians carved bracelets and other jewelry from this type of shell.

Flowers grow among the ancient stone walls of an Indian ruin, probably dating from ca. A.D. 1200, southern Arizona.

Snow blankets Tucson's San Xavier Mission, whose cathedral was constructed at the time of the American Revolution.

7

Exploration of the Deserts

European exploration of the deserts began by accident in 1535. A Spanish expedition had been shipwrecked on the Gulf coast of Texas in 1528, and four survivors under Alvar Nuñez Cabeza de Vaca wandered among the Indians for eight years. About 1535 they passed through parts of the Chihuahuan Desert, eventually reaching Spanish civilization in Mexico in 1536, where they reported rumors of magnificent Indian cities north of their route. A friar sent north to check these rumors in 1539 came back to Mexico City supporting the stories. Having just conquered the gold-laden Aztec and Inca empires, the Spanish conquistadors assumed another fabulous civilization awaited them. Coronado organized a massive army and traveled north in 1540, only to find that the fabled cities of gold were merely the poor adobe pueblos of New Mexico, where there was not enough turquoise to interest the soldiers. Further exploration was delayed until colonies were started in New Mexico around 1600.

Abandoned miners' cabins are common in desert mountain ranges. Gila Wilderness, New Mexico.

The greatest pioneer of the Sonoran Desert was Father Eusebio Kino, a hearty traveler of Italian stock who journeyed by horse and by foot through much of the region in the years around 1700. He founded the still-functioning, picturesque, mission San Xavier del Bac, among Indian villages in a fertile valley that is now Tucson, Arizona. He discovered multi-story Indian ruins, such as that near Casa Grande Arizona, and promoted the fertility of the region for settlement. His reports of the region's potential may strike a current visitor as overly enthusiastic, but we must remember that, in a sense, he saw a more fertile region than we do; the modern cities of Phoenix and Tucson, and associated modern agriculture, have pumped most of the water from the ground, lowering the water table, drying the rivers, and killing the abundant trees that lined the flowing streams of those days.

Colonization started in earnest not so much because of Kino's enthusiasm, but because of rich silver strikes just south of the border in 1736. Ever since, mining of ores including silver, gold, and especially copper, has been an important economic factor in the region.

One of the great expeditions of American history led to the crossing of the Sonoran Desert and the edge of the Mojave Deserts in order to reach California. Captain Juan Bautista de Anza left Arizona in 1775 with a vast party including 240 people, 695 horses and mules, and 355 cattle. The journey was successful and the expedition traveled up the California

Dilapidated wooden shacks are common in desert regions where mineral wealth once lured prospectors. This one is in desolate hills in southwestern Arizona, at "Charley Bell Well."

coast and founded the city of San Francisco.

The Mojave and Great Basin deserts were slower to be explored. In spite of some sporadic Spanish incursions, the first real exploration of the Great Basin came with the 1843 and 1845 expeditions of John C. Fremont. Fremont gave the name Great Basin. Although he was wrong in picturing it as one single basin, the name correctly implies the internal drainage of the area into various lakes. Because the drainage carries dissolved minerals into these lakes, many of them are salty, the most famous being the Great Salt Lake. This early knowledge of the region led to settlements in Utah by the Mormons, a religious sect that had come under for fire for a belief that included polygamy and the idea that American Indians represented a lost tribe of Israel. By a quirk of history, the neighboring state of Nevada, heart of the Great Basin desert, became a desert playground for California, so that the state with the strongest formal religion borders the state with the most legalized gambling and prostitution.

The Gold Rush of the mid 1800s drove many "'49ers" across the Western deserts. In particular, a southern route crossed the formidable deserts of the US-Mexico border region, where hundreds of travelers died due to the extreme conditions. Lonely, rocky graves still dot this route, but the Gold Rush era completed the opening of the Desert West and essentially ended the era of exploration.

Early settlers brought odd variants of Victorian architecture to desert towns in the 1800s. This example is in Fredonia, Arizona.

Rock crosses mark the graves of '49ers who didn't make it across the Sonoran Desert. Cabeza Prieta Wildlife Refuge, Arizona.

In the 1850s, the U.S. military attempted to introduce camels into the Southwest for transportation, under the direction of an Arab camel master, Haiji Ali. Ali's grave in western Arizona commemorates this unusual bit of desert history.

Buzzards congregating in a tree were an ill omen for stranded desert travelers.

A horse parade in Death Valley National Monument, California, looks like a scene from a John Ford Western.

8

The Mystique
of the Desert

The desert has long had a mystical fascination for humanity. Some of the world's major religions came out of Middle Eastern desert landscapes remarkably like the American deserts. At the turn of the century English explorers popularized this mystic lure of desert regions. One of the most famous, T. E. Lawrence (Lawrence of Arabia) wrote: "The creed of the desert seem(s) inexpressible in words ... (The) desert was made a spiritual icehouse, in which was preserved intact but unimproved for all ages a vision of the unity of God. This faith of the desert was impossible in the towns. It was at once too strange, too simple ...."

The uniqueness of desert life echoes in a newer generation of American desert writers, emerging especially in the Southwest. In books such as *Blue Desert, On the Mesa,* and *The Desert Smells Like Rain,* '80s writers Charles Bowden, John Nichols, and Gary Nabhan have forged a free-flowing form of non-fiction narrative as they tell of their own

Rapid erosion has produced a mud-walled labyrinth, in Cathedral Gorge State Park, Utah.

The pool at the base of Mooney Falls, Havasu Canyon, is a favorite spot for hikers who have crossed a dry desert valley to reach the site. Havasu Indian Reservation, Arizona.

encounters with the desert. In fiction, the desert lands perhaps have yet to emerge as inspiring a unique genre. Of course, writers from Zane Grey to Louis L'Amour have developed the western, but the western genre ranges throughout the whole west, from desert to mountain to prairie grassland, and looks back to a vanished past. Fiction writers such as John Nichols, Susan Lowell, Barbara Kinsolver, and Tony Hillerman are developing a more contemporary voice of life's experience in modern desert America.

All desert writers draw on an earlier wealth of American desert literature including non-fiction classics such as Mary Austin's *The Land of Little Rain* (1903) and Joseph Wood Krutch's *The Desert Year* (1952). One obscure turn-of-the-century classic is emerging into a renewed popularity. It is a peculiar book called simply *The Desert*, published in 1901. Its author, John C. Van Dyke, was an asthmatic Rutgers University art historian who decided, improbably, that a lonesome desert journey might improve his health. In the summer of 1897 he set out with a horse, a dog, a gun, a gallon of water, a few camping items, and no specific goal, from the present site of San Bernardino, California, heading into the oven of the Mojave Desert. He found that he was "alone without necessarily being lonesome." He advocated what he called "sensuous seeing," which meant combining sensitivity with knowledge. What he saw overwhelmed him. In poetic prose, Van Dyke's chapters describe desert light, air, desert skies, illusions, plants, animals, birds, mountains, and rivers. An intriguing mystery is Van Dyke's exact route; he kept no clear record of it, and often did not know his exact whereabouts. We know only that he traveled through much of the Mojave and Sonoran deserts, dipping occasionally into Mexico. He remarked that "The love of Nature is an acquired taste. One begins by admiring the Hudson River landscape and ends by loving the desolation of the Sahara." This is a progression many Americans have followed as they move from the East to the sun-belt western deserts.

Desert influences on the arts come from even older traditions. While trendy Anglo artists have often tended to follow influences of the East and West Coasts instead of developing an identifiably desert style, Native American artists' work in jewelry, ceramics, rugs, and paintings are seen in homes, museums, and social gatherings worldwide, and have been copied by designers and advertisers from New York to Los Angeles and abroad.

The mystique of the American desert speaks not only through its arts, but through the ancient traditions of its Native American inhabitants. In an age of environmental problems, the desert-dwellers' philosophy of simple living, minimal consumption instead of conspicuous consumption, and of brotherhood and sisterhood with the lifeforms and natural elements of the desert, is resonating ever more forcefully with our emerging ideas of how civilization can achieve harmony with the whole planet.

A classic vista from a desert highway: a storm over southern Utah.

Color contrasts in the view through a natural bridge, Bryce Canyon National Park, Utah.

Zion Ledge, Zion National Park, Utah.

El Tovar is one of the grand old hotels of the National Park system.

Native Americans selling finely made turquoise jewelry and other craft items are a common sight along desert highways through reservations. New Mexico.

Many early and contemporary Southwest buildings, such as this New Mexico village house, use adobe bricks made from local materials.

A vertical view of an arch in the "Fiery Furnace" at Arches National Park, Utah.

Sand dunes add to the picturesqueness of eroded sandstone towers in Monument Valley, Utah.

Late afternoon light catches the peaks of Mt. Wrightson, southern Arizona, while the valley is already in shadow.
Such scenes are common in the basin and range province, where valleys fall into shadow while the ridges catch the last light.

Several desert mountain ranges are topped by astronomical observatories,
because the desert offers clear air, away from the lights and smog of large cities.

Grasslands at the contact between the Sonoran and Chihuahuan deserts, near Dragoon, southeast Arizona.

A round-trip mule ride along the Kaibab Trail is one of the traditional attractions of Grand Canyon National Park.

Agricultural fields on the Zuni Indian Reservations.

9

Modern Life in the Desert

John Van Dyke wrote that the deserts are "the breathing-spaces of the west." But, he warned, "...to speak about sparing anything because it is beautiful is to waste one's breath and incur ridicule in the bargain.... The aesthetic sense – the power to enjoy through the eye, the ear, and the imagination – is just as important ... as the corporeal sense of eating and drinking; but there never has been a time when the world would admit it ... have we not seen, here in California and Oregon, in our own time, the destruction of the fairest valleys the sun ever shone upon by placer and hydraulic mining?"

This sort of lament, voiced by Van Dyke as early as 1901, has been a constant refrain in America's desert country ever since.

Newcomers from more vegetated regions generally start their desert tenure by trying to recreate "back home" with green lawns and

Agricultural irrigation canals support striking green fields in the otherwise "barren" desert. Western Arizona.

Changing fortunes, water tables, and climates have left many abandoned ranches in the desert region of the West, such as this example in Utah.

trees. Resulting water consumption has lowered water tables, altered vegetation patterns, and led to a battle for water throughout the dry parts of the West.

Irrigation has helped the modern American miracle of food production, and yet has turned into a complex problem. Irrigation uses even more water per acre than urban growth, thus fueling a controversy about the value of desert agriculture. Developers, meanwhile, eager to cash in on the desire for Sun Belt housing, have enormously expanded American desert cities such as Phoenix, Tucson, Las Vegas, Palm Springs, and Salt Lake City. Urban sprawl has generally been along the river valleys, thus eating up the highest quality agricultural soils, a dubious accomplishment in view of world hunger problems. In turn, the unusually rapid urban growth has left many modern desert cities hard-pressed to keep up with growing problems of traffic and smog that invariably accompany urban expansion. In response to these problems, citizen involvement in planning and zoning issues, and a tendency to make developers (and ultimately new home buyers) share more of the costs of desert urban growth have led to some improvement in the aesthetic and practical design of several desert cities in recent years.

The problems of expanding population also impact on the natural environment around desert cities. Deserts are much more fragile than, for example, eastern woodlands. A road cut in the East will be covered by new vegetation in a few years, while a similar road cut in the desert remains a visible scar for many years. Thus, every disturbance, from a dune buggy driver's swath through a cactus patch to a failed housing development, leaves damage visible for a generation or more. The intrusion of huge new cities in only a generation, coupled with the ability of desert enthusiasts to get into the wilderness in off-road vehicles, has led to unprecedented stress on the delicate desert. New legislation has prohibited or strictly limited such practices as poaching cacti for home landscaping, digging up ancient artifacts, and hunting. During the last five decades, for example, the Sonoran Desert strip along the southwest Arizona border went from the status of open range for hunting and cattle grazing, to the status of Game Range and then to the that of Wildlife Refuge. The population of bighorn sheep, which had dipped from hundreds to as low as 50, is back up to around 400 as a result of these conservation measures.

The message for the future is clear. New residents will continue to be attracted by the dry climates, many of which are warm and free of heavy snow. But rampant unplanned urban development must cease because of the fragility of this environment. The desert will ask its citizens to educate themselves as to its special challenges. The desert will require us not merely to accept the growth patterns fostered by economic forces, but to work together to choose the patterns of community growth that will allow us all to preserve the special attractions of desert life.

The power needs of distant cities have brought some smoke pollution to the shore of Lake Powell.

Dusk in Arches National Monument, Utah.

Bright Angel Trail, Grand Canyon National Park, Arizona.

Havasu Canyon, Grand Canyon National Park.

Increased tourist pressure on natural recreation areas has led to their closure to cars and access only by tram services.
While some visitor are dismayed, joggers and bikers find the car-free park roads inviting.

Breaking camp at Cabeza Prietas at dawn.

One of the charms of desert city life in the Southwest is the contrast between old Spanish styles and modern urban architecture.

A river runner challenges the waves on the Yampa River, Utah.
River running is a favorite sport among parched desert dwellers.

Big horn sheep were widely depicted in ancient rock art. The population dwindled at the turn
of the century due to big game hunting, but has recovered in some wildlife refuge areas.

Occasional vapor trails may be the only sign of modern life
to be seen from many remote desert locations.

Hiking trails treat nature lovers to striking vistas at every turn in Zion National Park, Utah.

The beehive oven using native materials is of ancient design. It is an element of "Santa Fe style" and is common in many New Mexico homes. Pecos National Monument, New Mexico.

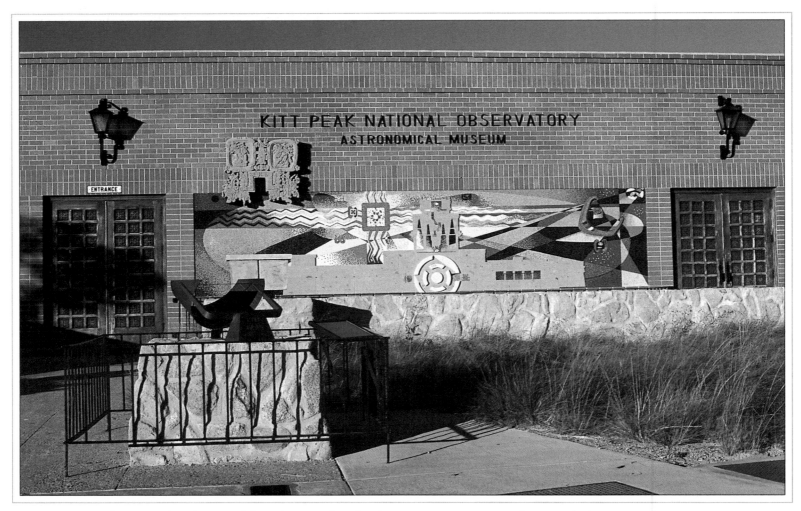

Ancient and modern motifs have been combined in the visitor center at Kitt Peak National Observatory, Arizona.

The clear skies of southwest deserts have led to interest in hot air ballooning.
Here, a balloon takes to the skies during a rally over the outskirts of Tucson, Arizona.

The open vistas and distant horizons of the deserts produce sunsets famous the world over.

Anasazi steps beside the San Juan River, Utah.